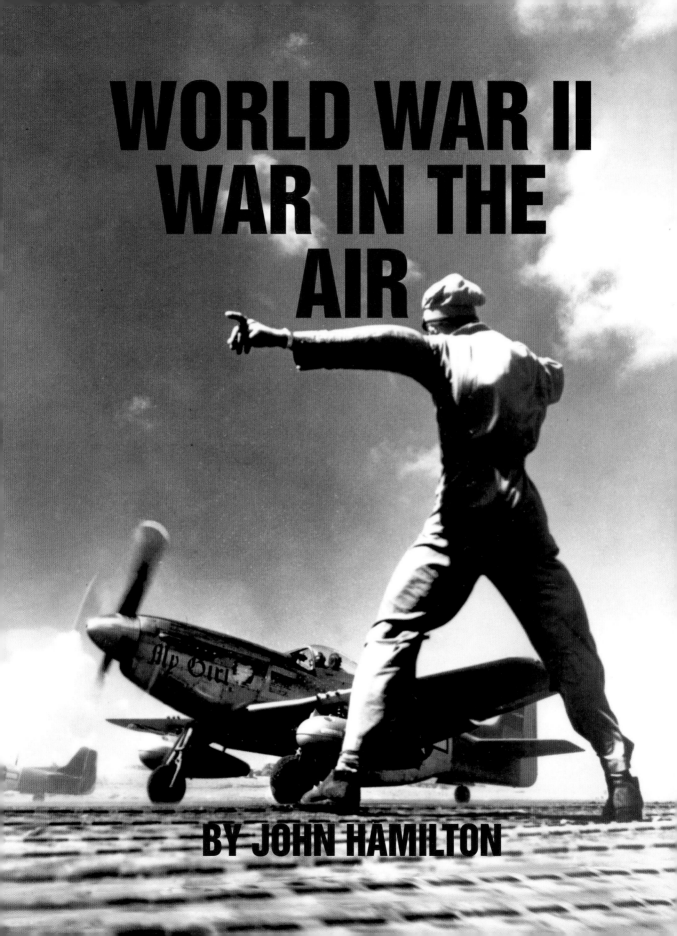

WORLD WAR II
WAR IN THE AIR

BY JOHN HAMILTON

VISIT US AT
WWW.ABDOPUBLISHING.COM

Published by ABDO Publishing Company, 8000 West 78th Street, Suite 310, Edina, MN 55439. Copyright ©2012 by Abdo Consulting Group, Inc. International copyrights reserved in all countries. No part of this book may be reproduced in any form without written permission from the publisher. ABDO & Daughters™ is a trademark and logo of ABDO Publishing Company.

Printed in the United States of America, North Mankato, Minnesota.
082011
092011

♻ PRINTED ON RECYCLED PAPER

Editor: Sue Hamilton
Graphic Design: John Hamilton
Cover Design: Neil Klinepier
Cover Photo: National Archives and Records Administration (NARA)
Interior Photos and Illustrations: Alamy-pgs 10 & 11; AP-pg 7 (middle); Corbis-pgs 9 & 12; Digital Stock-pgs 3, 14-15, 22-23 & 31; Getty Images-pgs 7 (bottom), 8, 13, 15 (inset), 16-17, 20, 21, 26, 27, 28, & 29; Granger Collection-pgs 5 & 6; iStockphoto-pg 7; NARA-pg 4; U.S. Air Force-pgs 1, 9 (top), 18, 19, 24 & 25; and U.S. Navy-pg 9 (middle).

ABDO Booklinks

To learn more about World War II, visit ABDO Publishing Company online. Web sites about World War II are featured on our Book Links pages. These links are routinely monitored and updated to provide the most current information available. Web site: www.abdopublishing.com

Library of Congress Cataloging-in-Publication Data

Hamilton, John, 1959-
  World War II : war in the air / John Hamilton.
    p. cm. -- (World War II)
  Includes index.
  ISBN 978-1-61783-063-1
  1. World War, 1939-1945--Aerial operations--Juvenile literature. I. Title.
  D785.H35 2012
  940.54'4--dc23
                        2011020134

CONTENTS

WAR IN THE AIR

American dive bombers over Japan.

Airpower changed the face of warfare during World War II. Its impact was enormous. Both sides used planes to spy on the enemy. Fast fighters preyed on ground troops and convoys. Powerful bombers flew hundreds of miles deep into enemy territory to attack factories, oil refineries, railways, and entire cities.

Many planes from World War II are legendary: Mustangs and Flying Fortresses from the United States; Spitfires and Hurricanes from the United Kingdom; Zeroes from Japan; and Stukas and Messerschmitts from Germany. All these planes had different jobs to do. Most did their work with deadly accuracy. Some became obsolete in just a few short years. All played a major role in their countries' war efforts.

Airpower helped win the war for the Allies, but it also had a dark side. For the first time in history, both sides targeted civilians on purpose on a massive scale. The bombing and destruction of cities was meant to shorten the war. Hundreds of thousands of innocent people were the victims of this military strategy. It is a terrible legacy of airpower during World War II.

A B-17 Flying Fortress loses half its tail section during a bombing mission over Germany.

GERMAN
AIR POWER

Junkers dive bomber

When World War II began in 1939, Nazi Germany had the most powerful air force in the world. Called the *Luftwaffe*, it was created mainly to support ground troops and armored vehicles. The Nazis used this "combined arms" tactic very effectively in *blitzkrieg* ("lightning warfare) attacks against countries such as Poland and France.

The Junkers Ju 87 "Stuka" dive bomber was an early symbol of blitzkrieg attacks. It made a distinctive screeching noise when it dove toward its targets. Although effective early in the war, it was slow and not very maneuverable.

The Messerschmitt Bf 109 was Germany's best fighter. It had a top speed of 435 miles per hour (684 kph), and was very effective at intercepting enemy fighters as well as bombing ground targets.

The Luftwaffe did not make very many heavy bombers. Its most important bombers included the Heinkel He 111 and the Dornier Do 17, nicknamed the "flying pencil." Although fast, they couldn't carry very many bombs. This hurt Germany's chances for victory in the last years of the war.

Messerschmitt Bf 109 fighter

Heinkel He 111 bomber

A view out of a Heinkel's cabin.

Dornier Do 17 "flying pencil" bomber

JAPANESE
AIR POWER

Mitsubishi Zero

During World War II, Japan wanted to expand its empire over a huge section of Asia, including a wide area of the Pacific Ocean. To do this, it relied a great deal on aircraft carriers. Several of these massive ships were used on Japan's successful sneak attack on the American naval base at Pearl Harbor, Hawaii.

The most famous of Japan's planes was the Mitsubishi A6M "Zero." At the beginning of the war, fast and agile Zeros ruled the skies over the Pacific. Toward the end of the war, however, Zeros were outclassed by newer American planes, and their weak defenses resulted in many being shot down in dogfights.

Other famous Japanese planes included the Aichi D3 "Val" dive bomber and the Nakajima B5N2 "Kate" torpedo bomber. Like Germany, Japan didn't rely very much on long-range heavy bombers. The country's most famous twin-engine bomber was the Mitsubishi G4M "Betty." It had a range of 2,700 miles (4,345 km), but was easy to shoot down because of its unprotected fuel tanks.

"Val" dive bomber

"Kate" torpedo bomber

Mitsubishi "Betty" bomber

9

SOVIET UNION
AIR POWER

Yakovlev "Yak" fighter

During the early years of World War II, the Soviet Union did not have a very effective air force. The VVS (Voenno-Vozdushnye Sily—"Military Air Forces") lacked experienced pilots and ground crews. Also, planes and equipment were destroyed when the German army invaded the Soviet Union in 1941.

As the war dragged on, Soviet factories produced thousands of new combat aircraft. One of the most important planes was the Ilyushin IL-2, which was made by the tens of thousands. It was very effective at attacking German armored vehicles and ground troops.

The Yakovlev Yak-1 fighter, and later versions, gained air superiority over the German Luftwaffe toward the end of the war. German pilots were eventually ordered to avoid combat with the fast and powerful Yaks.

The Soviet Union was the only country that allowed women to fly combat missions. Pilots of the 588th Night Bomber Regiment were nicknamed the "Night Witches." They were highly skilled and daring. Many female pilots flew more than 1,000 missions against Germany.

Ilyushin IL-2 "flying tank" ground-attack aircraft

The Soviet Union's female combat pilots were called "Stalin's Falcons" and "Night Witches."

BRITISH
AIR POWER

Hurricane fighter

The British Royal Air Force (RAF) was created in 1918. It is the world's oldest independent air force. Before World War II, the United Kingdom was more well known for its powerful Royal Navy. During the war, however, the RAF played a major part in saving the British Isles from being invaded by Nazi Germany.

The most famous British planes were the Hawker Hurricane and Supermarine Spitfire. The Hurricane was a fighter that was later used to attack ground targets. The famous Spitfire was extremely maneuverable, able to win dogfights against almost any German plane. Both aircraft had powerful Rolls-Royce engines.

In addition to its successful fighter aircraft, the United Kingdom also produced long-range bombers. The Avro Lancaster was a four-engine heavy bomber with a range of 2,530 miles (4,072 km). These planes flew many missions deep inside German territory, especially at night.

Spitfire fighter

Lancaster bomber

13

The BATTLE OF BRITAIN

In 1940, Germany's Adolf Hitler wanted to invade the United Kingdom. But for the German army to cross the English Channel safely on ships, it would first have to control the skies.

In July 1940, the first waves of German aircraft attacked RAF airfields and radar units. They also attacked coastal shipping and aircraft factories.

At first, the RAF was outnumbered and outgunned. But as the weeks dragged on, British Hurricane and Spitfire fighters shot down German fighters and bombers by the hundreds. The Germans changed their strategy to bombing British cities at night.

After weeks of fighting, the Germans finally abandoned their plan to invade the United Kingdom. The battle was costly for both sides. The Germans lost almost 1,900 aircraft and 2,700 aircrew members. More than 1,500 British aircraft were shot down, with a loss of about 544 pilots and aircrew.

After the German invasion threat was foiled, Prime Minister Winston Churchill praised the bravery of the RAF pilots. In a speech to the House of Commons on August 20, 1940, he said, "Never in the field of human conflict was so much owed by so many to so few."

British pilots "scramble" to their planes during a German air raid.

Parts of London burn after German planes bomb the city.

AMERICAN
AIR POWER

After being attacked by Japan in 1941, the United States used its vast industrial might to produce an air force unmatched anywhere in the world.

The United States Army Air Forces (renamed the United States Air Force in 1947) used several kinds of planes in the war in Europe against Nazi Germany. The Boeing B-17 Flying Fortress was a four-engine heavy bomber with a range of 1,095 miles (1,762 km) fully loaded with bombs. Thousands of B-17s were built during the war. They flew in large groups, usually in precision daylight bombing raids against German military and industrial targets.

To protect the bombers, the U.S. used fighters to dogfight enemy planes. The best fighter of the war was the North American P-51 Mustang. It used a special "drop tank" with extra fuel mounted on its belly so that it could escort the B-17s deep into German territory. Grateful bomber crews called the Mustang their "little friend."

Another famous American fighter was the Lockheed P-38 Lightning, a twin-engine fighter with an unusual double fuselage. It had heavy weapons mounted in its nose, and could carry up to 4,000 pounds (1,814 kg) of bombs to attack ground targets. The Germans called it the "fork-tailed devil."

P-51 Mustangs

B-17 bomber

P-38 Lightning fighter

THE MEMPHIS BELLE

The *Memphis Belle* was the nickname of a B-17 Flying Fortress that made 25 complete bombing missions with a single crew. Usually, B-17 missions were so dangerous that at least one third of the crew were expected to be killed or wounded. The average age of most crews was just 20 years old.

Pilot Robert Morgan named the aircraft in honor of his girlfriend, Margaret Polk, of Memphis, TN. Between November 1942 and May 1943, Polk and his crew flew bombing missions over France, the Netherlands, Belgium, and Germany. Every major part of the plane was repaired or replaced at least once because of battle damage.

After flying 25 missions, B-17 crews were eligible to be reassigned in the United States. Once back home, the *Memphis Belle* and its crew crisscrossed the nation promoting the sale of war bonds. The plane became very famous, and was the subject of many books, a 1944 documentary, and a 1990 Hollywood movie.

The *Memphis Belle* is now at the National Museum of the U.S. Air Force at Wright-Patterson Air Force Base in Dayton, Ohio.

The crew of the B-17 Flying Fortress Memphis Bell *at an English air base after successfully completing 25 missions over enemy territory.*

PARATROOPERS

Paratroopers in World War II were elite soldiers dropped into enemy territory to capture important targets such as airstrips, roadways, and bridges. During the drop, the round parachutes could be steered slightly by pulling on straps connected to the canopy. Even so, paratroopers sometimes landed in trees or water hazards and were injured or killed.

Paratroopers had the element of surprise, but once on the ground they did not have support from heavy guns or armored vehicles.

In 1940, Germany used paratroopers to capture airfields in Norway. And in May 1941, German paratroopers captured an airfield on the Greek island of Crete in the Mediterranean Sea. It was a costly victory: the paratroopers suffered almost 7,000 casualties.

The Allies used paratroopers during the Normandy invasion in France. Thousands of American and British airborne troops were dropped by silent gliders behind enemy lines the night before D-Day, June 6, 1944. Many paratroopers were killed or injured, but they succeeded in capturing key bridges and roads.

The largest airborne action of the war was Operation Market Garden. About 42,000 American and British paratroopers were dropped into the German-occupied Netherlands in September 1944.

American paratroopers prepare to jump into Normandy, France.

AIRCRAFT
CARRIERS

The Japanese and American navies relied heavily on aircraft carriers for control of the far-flung islands of the Pacific Ocean. The largest aircraft carriers, such as the American Essex-class USS *Yorktown*, were 869 feet (265 m) long, more than 2.5 times the length of a football field. They could hold 90-100 planes, and carried a crew of 3,448.

Some of the earliest U.S. carrier-based airplanes were Grumman F4F Wildcats. Because they could take off from short runways, they were used on many of the smaller aircraft carriers. Wildcats had a top speed of 318 miles per hour (512 kph). Later in the war, they were replaced by faster and more agile F6F Hellcats.

Chance-Vought F4U Corsairs were among the best carrier-based planes of World War II. These gull-wing fighter-bombers had a top speed of 417 miles per hour (671 kph) and could outmaneuver any enemy plane. The Japanese called them "whistling death."

Carrier-based airpower was so effective that battleships became less important. In the Battle of the Coral Sea in May 1942, the Americans and Japanese hammered each other's ships with swarms of carrier-based aircraft. For the first time in history, the opposing ships never saw each other. The battle was a victory for the United States.

Above: An American SB2C dive bomber circles around to land on the aircraft carrier USS *Yorktown*.

THE DOOLITTLE RAID

A B-25 takes off from the deck of the aircraft carrier USS *Hornet*.

On the morning of April 18, 1942, just four months after the devastating Japanese attack on the United States naval base at Pearl Harbor, Hawaii, 16 B-25 Mitchell twin-engine bombers took off from the flight deck of the USS *Hornet* in the western Pacific Ocean.

The *Hornet* had sailed within 750 miles (1,207 km) of Japan. Now the B-25s and their 80 crewmen, led by Lieutenant Colonel James Doolittle, would make a daring strike on the enemy's homeland.

After six hours of flying at wave-top level to avoid detection, the B-25s arrived at the Japanese capital of Tokyo and several other cities and dropped their bombs. Because they were running low on fuel, the planes then flew on to China. Most of the crewmen parachuted out over Japanese-controlled territory. They safely made it home thanks to the brave help of Chinese soldiers and civilians.

The Japanese people were told by their leaders that they were invulnerable to attack. Doolittle's raid caused confusion and anger. In addition, even though the raid did little significant damage to the enemy, it was a huge boost to American morale.

Lieutenant Colonel James Doolittle (left) stands with the skipper of the USS *Hornet*, Captain Marc Mitscher.

The aircraft carrier *Hornet* had 16 B-25 bombers on deck, ready for the raid on Tokyo, Japan.

STRATEGIC BOMBING

The United States and the United Kingdom built their air forces around the idea of "strategic bombing." By using four-engine heavy bombers that flew deep into enemy territory, they could attack German factories, shipyards, railways, and other military targets. The Germans would be forced to surrender, the theory went, because their ability to wage war would be crippled.

The German and Japanese air forces also used strategic bombing. The Germans tried for months to demoralize the British public with the "Blitz," the nighttime bombing of London and other cities. The Japanese bombed many Chinese cities.

To help with precision bombing, American B-17 Flying Fortresses were fitted with top-secret Norden bombsights. These were computer-like devices that helped the planes' bombardiers decide exactly when to release their bombs. It was said that by using the Norden bombsight, American air crews could "drop a bomb in a pickle barrel."

London during the Blitz.

American B-26 Marauders bomb a German railway yard.

Allied bombing created a firestorm in the historic German city of Dresden that killed at least 25,000 civilians.

Unfortunately, the Norden bombsight wasn't as accurate in practice as was hoped. Many bombs missed their mark. Even when factories and other targets were hit, they were soon rebuilt. Germany's war output was not hurt enough to make the country surrender. While the Americans continued with precision daylight bombing, the British Royal Air Force switched to nighttime bombing of German cities. The Americans also sometimes bombed cities. Civilians were deliberately attacked with the hope of shortening the war.

From about 1943 to 1945, many German cities were bombed, resulting in hundreds of thousands of deaths and injuries. Cities such as Dresden, Hamburg, Kassel, and Mainz were reduced to rubble. In July 1943, a firestorm in Hamburg alone killed more than 42,000 civilians. With strategic bombing coupled with Allied ground attacks, Germany finally surrendered in May 1945.

In Japan, American bombers were relentless. B-29 Superfortress heavy bombers raided Japanese cities night after night. The firebombing of Tokyo left at least 100,000 dead.

On August 6 and 9, 1945, B-29s dropped atomic bombs on the cities of Hiroshima and Nagasaki. These single bombs completely destroyed the cities. On August 15, the Japanese finally surrendered.

A Japanese city on the island of Honshu is engulfed in a firestorm.

The power and force of strategic bombing shocked the world. There is much debate whether it actually shortened the war or simply increased the level of misery and destruction. One fact is undeniable: thanks in large part to airpower, more innocent civilians were killed during World War II than in any war in human history.

A test firing of an atomic bomb taken 16 milliseconds after detonation.

GLOSSARY

AIR RAID

The dropping of bombs from a military aircraft aimed at a city, factory, or other specific target on the ground.

ALLIES

The Allies were the many nations that were allied, or joined, in the fight against Germany, Italy, and Japan in World War II. The most powerful nations among the Allies included the United States, Great Britain, the Soviet Union, France, China, and Canada.

BLITZKRIEG

A German word meaning "lightning warfare." It described a new strategy that the German military used in World War II. *Blitzkrieg* called for very large invasions to overwhelm the enemy quickly with combined land and air attacks in order to avoid long, drawn-out battles.

CASUALTY

Soldiers and civilians reported as either killed, wounded, or missing in action.

D-DAY

A day when a military operation begins. Most people today associate D-Day with the Normandy invasion of June 6, 1944.

FIGHTER

A small, fast plane that is used to battle other planes in the air. Fighters were often used to escort large and slow bomber planes over enemy territory.

FIREBOMBING

Deliberate bombing of targets with incendiary devices, which spread uncontrollable fires. Much more damage can potentially be inflicted on a target, especially a city, with firebombing than with simple explosive bombs. Many British, German, and Japanese cities were firebombed during World War II. This kind of strategic bombing was meant to demoralize the enemy's populace and hasten the end of the war.

HEAVY BOMBER

A bomber capable of carrying large numbers of bombs great distances.

NAZI

The Nazi Party was the political party in Germany that supported Adolf Hitler. After 1934 it was the only political party allowed in Germany. This is when Hitler became a dictator and ruled Germany with total power.

A Grumman F6F Hellcat fighter prepares to take off from the USS *Yorktown*.

INDEX